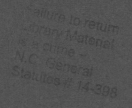

A POEM FOR PETER

ANDREA DAVIS PINKNEY
pictures by LOU FANCHER & STEVE JOHNSON

A POEM FOR PETER

The Story of
EZRA JACK KEATS
and the Creation of
THE SNOWY DAY

VIKING

This book is dedicated to Jerry Pinkney —A. D. P.

✳

For Ezra Jack Keats and the people of all ages
who love his books —L. F. and S. J.

BROWN-SUGAR BOY in a blanket of white.
Bright as the day you came onto the page.
From the hand of a man who saw you for you.

Long before *you* arrived,
little brown-sugar child, *he* was born.
Came to this world
in the middle of March
that time between a lion and a lamb.

Yes, yes, *he* was born with a roar
that would someday celebrate
the making
of a brown-sugar boy on a snowy day.

You and *he*,
different,
but the same in so many ways.

This wriggly baby
was the youngest of three.
First came sister Mae, a feisty girl.
Then brother Willie, a quiet dreamer.
Then came *he*.

Jacob

(Jack)

Ezra

Katz

Born under Hardship's Hand,
into a land filled with impossible odds.

His parents, Benjamin and Gussie,
were Polish immigrants.
Each fled Warsaw.
Benjamin first.
Then Gussie.

Journeyed westward on a big boat
packed tight with others like them,
wanting a new life.

Bound for America,
where, they prayed,
no one would prey
on Jews as they'd done back in Poland.

They leapt onto American soil.
Eyes filled with expectation.
Looking to see.
This Home of the Free.
This United States land of opportunity.

Benjamin and Gussie
settled in Brooklyn,
where they had to hunt
for what was good.

There wasn't much prospect
in this Brooklyn place.
Jobs—scarce.
Poverty—plenty.

The dark heel of
Discrimination—
dancing in the streets
of what was now their home:
East New York,
Brooklyn's poorest part of town,
in 1916,
when Jacob (Jack) Ezra Katz
was born.

But when it snowed,
oh, when it snowed!
Nature's glittery hand
painted the world's walls a brighter shade.

Snow made opportunity and equality
seem right around the corner.
Because, you see, Snow is nature's *we-all* blanket.
When Snow spreads her sheet, *we all* glisten.
When Snow paints the streets, *we all* see her beauty.

Snow doesn't know who's needy or dirty
or greedy or nice.
Snow doesn't *choose* where to fall.
Snow doesn't pick a wealthy man's doorstep
over a poor lady's stoop.
That's Snow's magic.

13

Benjamin Katz made meager wages
as a waiter at Pete's Coffee Pot
in Greenwich Village.

Every day Ezra's daddy served
and smiled for the busy city people
who didn't always tip
this hardworking man,
his apron stained with fry-grease
and the longing for something better
than his battered flat on Vermont Street.

Ma Gussie was a strong-willed woman
with a paintbrush she mostly kept secret.
Ma Gussie,
a mother with hushed-up wishes
of becoming a *fine* artist.
Fine—as in cultured.
Fine—as in *re*fined.
Fine—as in beauty for beauty's sake.

But Ma Gussie could never
utter her *fine-fine* wishes.
She was forced to bite down
on her dreams.
This made her bitter,
a way Ezra never wanted to be.

When Ezra turned eight,
he took a page
from life's book of hard wanting.
He swiped a sheet of what it might mean
to become an artist,
that unutterable thing.

As a third grader at P.S. 182,
Ezra earned twenty-five cents
for painting store signs.
His hand so steady,
ready to show what he could do
with a brush dipped in gold,
spelling, spiraling,
inviting shoppers to buy:
PIGS' FEET & SAUERKRAUT—25¢
PANCAKES & SAUSAGES—15¢

With shiny dimes pressed into his palm,
Ezra Katz learned he had a gift for
creating something that made people look.
This was the answer to
Papa Benjamin's prayers.

His son could earn good money
as a sign painter.

But the child was cut from the patches of
his mother's cloth.
He wanted to be a *true* artist.

True—as in the real thing.
True—as in letting imagination fly.
True—as in someone who does more
than paint sauerkraut signs.

Papa Benjamin worried
about his son's dream.
Feared for what he couldn't see.
An artist was a strange, impractical
thing to be.
You couldn't earn a decent wage
giving imagination wings.

But even with these firm beliefs,
Papa Benjamin had a soft spot.
He brought home
half-used tubes of paint
from artists who hung around
at Pete's Coffee Pot.

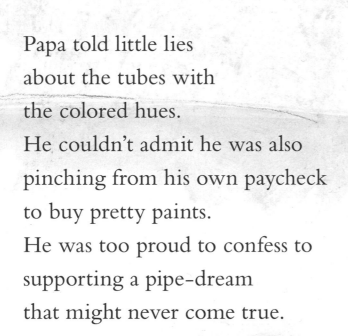

With each tube of colored oil,
Ezra let his imagination grow.
And he drew, oh, how he drew.
On paper bags.
And wood scraps.
And box tops.
And pillowcases.
And open palms.
And foot-soles.

Papa told little lies
about the tubes with
the colored hues.
He couldn't admit he was also
pinching from his own paycheck
to buy pretty paints.
He was too proud to confess to
supporting a pipe-dream
that might never come true.

Ezra's teachers helped
his art-star shine.
He spent school days
cutting, pasting, making collages.
Gluing torn swatches.
Squirting his oils onto sheets
and sheets,
onto *please, oh, please,
keep-feeding-me-these.*

Thank goodness for teachers.
Thank goodness for friends.
Loved that boy, yes they did.
Saw his gifts, before he could.

Teachers and friends, oh, how they *did*.
Teachers and friends, oh, how they *could*.
Bring out the good—the best of the best—
in Jacob (Jack) Ezra Katz.

Told Ezra—*You've got a knack.*
Encouraged him—*Don't hold it back.*
Took Jacob (Jack) Ezra Katz by the hand,
like a pair of warm mittens,
and led him to a place of promise:
The Brooklyn Public Library,
with its enchanted land
called the Reference Room.

Ezra spent afternoons
in that so-special place,
made an eager leap into heaps of happy.
Landed onto piles of pretty.

Art books!

Plant facts!

Bug tales!

Maps!

Pages and pages of pictures and paintings,
like the doors of that so-special place,
opened so wide,
invited, ignited Ezra's imagination:
Come, child, fly!

But with that bright art-star shine,
there soon came a CRASH!
The stock market—SMASHED!
The Great Depression—BAM!—
came on with a punch.
Brought hard knocks.
Brought bad times.
Made the poor even poorer.
Made sad an even bleaker shade of gray.

By 1932, when he was a student
at Thomas Jefferson High School,
the kid was pulling in prizes
for his drawings, and murals,
and etchings, and oils.

Then came Ezra's *Shantytown*,
a painting that showed it like it was.
Let folks see, let them *feel*
what the Great Depression's heavy hand
had doled out: despair.

Shantytown brought citations, applause.
Helped Jacob (Jack) Ezra Katz
graduate with honors,
and scholarships to art school.

But on the day before Ezra's graduation,
Papa Benjamin died of a heart attack.
Ma Gussie sank into deep-blue darkness.

Ezra never got to wear
his cap and gown.
He kissed those scholarships a fast good-bye.
Oh, such Great Disappointment.
Out of school.
Out of work.
Out of luck.

Where to go?
How to know
which way to turn
when every avenue
is a dead-end street.

Odd jobs put pennies in Ezra's pocket.
Let him patch together a living.
Let him catch-as-catch-can.
Those patchy-catch pennies
paid the rent,
bought some bread.

Then, like a friend who shows up
with a gift,
the Art Students League said:
Come with me.
Handed Ezra a chance.

The Art Students League.
A playground for experimenting.
A schoolyard of inspiration
that introduced Ezra
to the paintings of Mexican greats:
Orozco,
Rivera,
Siqueiros.

In the midst of the Great Depression,
President Roosevelt promised
a brighter day.
Shook hands with Americans.
Made a pact.
Gave his word on what he called
The New Deal.
Spelled his promise with three letters:
WPA.
The Works Progress Administration.

What a boon for Ezra Katz.
The WPA meant a J-O-B.
The government paid artists to paint.
Catch-as-catch-can
became *paint-for-pay, good man!*

And so, Ezra painted murals
for the WPA.
After that, he found a job
as a comic-book artist.
He drew capes. And crowns.
And shields. And fists.
He sketched villains.
And marvels.
And heroes.
He inked. And colored.
And told stories in strips.

**And that, little child, brought _you_
one step closer.
Yes, Peter, _you._**

The brown-sugar boy
in a blanket of white
began to ignite by what kids saw,
and _didn't_ see,
in the not-so-funny comics
Ezra was made to draw.
All the heroes in _all_ the comics
were _always_ as white as a winter sky.

Peter, child, _you_ were so-not-anywhere
among any superheroes.
People wondered, _how could this be?_
Why weren't _you_ on the same pages
among the other marvels?

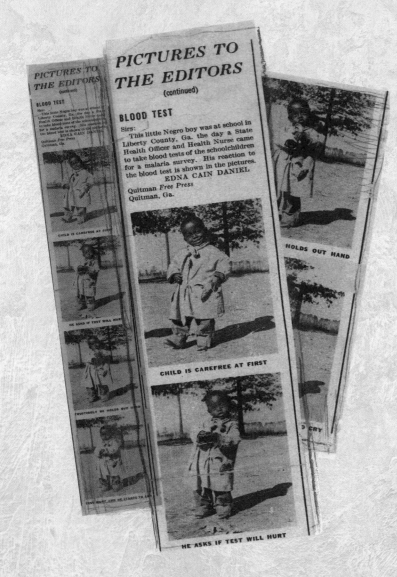

A roly-poly celebration.
A charming, chubby bundle
of boundlessness.
You jumped out in front of Ezra
in a series of photographs
from *Life* magazine.
Your sweet-cheeked smile brought
a sprinkle of joy.

Ezra tacked those *Life* magazine
brown-sugar goodies onto his wall,
where the photos would stay
for twenty years.

Even though the world was living
in an age of color judgment,
your color didn't matter to Ezra.
All he saw was *you*,
beguiling little guy,
with the smarty-pants smirk,
playing pretty-boy peek-a-boo.

But *you*, cocoa sprite,
weren't far away.
You, a funny kid
filled with brown-sugar whimsy.

An important thing happened
around this time.
War rose up throughout the world.
Hitler, an evil beast of a man,
was on a mission
to rid every crevice and country
of all Jews,
and anyone else born with even a drop
of difference.

Uncle Sam pointed his finger,
stared hard.
Told Ezra: *I Want You!*
Drafted him quick,
asked him to serve
the Red,
White,
and Blue.

Ezra went, proud to fight.
Eager to help end Hitler's reign.
Packed his pencils, brought his brushes,
marched to the army.
Took his soldier self
to the Air Force division,
and served Uncle Sam a big dose
of draftsmanship.

World War II needed posters
and booklets.
Needed charts.
Needed art.
Needed maps and pictures
drawn by the hand of a man whose
lines and arrows sprang from the page
to help soldiers leap to duty.

After the war,
Ezra did something many Jews did
when the want ads said:
"No Jews Need Apply."

To help himself get a job,
Jacob (Jack) Ezra Katz
rearranged his name.
Shortened that name,
twisted its rhythm.
Helped it roll off the tongue.

Yes, yes—*Ezra Jack Keats*.
Had a nicer ring to it—for some.
It was a name that only hinted at
   his heritage.
      Only winked at where he'd
      come from,
         but never came out and said.

33

Discrimination had formed Ezra's
understanding of what it meant to be
different.
This also led to *you*, brown-sugar boy.

Back in his hometown,
you gave a wave, once again.
Those *Life*-affirming photos teased Ezra.
They'd been twinkling hello
for so long,
waiting to *come* to *life*.
Soon to *change* Ezra's life—and ours.

One day Ezra was asked
to draw pictures
for a children's book called
Jubilant for Sure.
That was a very good year—1954.
It was a new beginning
for Ezra Jack Keats.

For sure,
making art for children's stories
was a jubilant reason to rejoice.

Okay, maybe so, but the delight
was *all white*.
The books on the shelves
made Ezra call out
like a daddy looking for his lost child:
Where are you?

And he *kept* calling, *kept* asking:

Where?
Are?
You?

And then, Ezra's invitation came
to write and illustrate his own story.
And then—oh, then—*you!*
You popped up!
You! Ezra's true jubilation.
You had been waiting to be born.
And yet, you were there all along.

35

Brown-sugar boy in a blanket of white.
Bright as the day you came onto the
page.
From the hand of a man
whose life and times,
and hardships,
and heritage,
and heroes,
and heart,
and soul
led him to *you*.

Yes, *you*, little boy,
were now in full view.
Peter!
No longer a glint in Ezra's eye,
but a curious child on a path
to discovery.

Like a snowflake you fell,
right into our hearts.
You arrived.
A little Snowy Day surprise!
Like a crystal flake from the clouds,
you fluttered down
with your own one-of-a-kind
cutie-beauty.

Yes, *you*, Peter child, bubbled up
in this man,
now free to discover
the truth of your colors:
The here-I-am Red.
The look-at-me Yellow.
The proud-to-be Brown.

Yes, *you*.
A bright-hooded hero,
snow-suited crusader,
crunching through your own
quiet tundra of discovery.

You, brown-sugar boy,
with your black-button eyes and hot-cocoa nose.
You, facing the cold, with your
matching mittens and tiny boots.

You, so cute,
like a brown snowman's child.

You, Peter, a tiny might,
were your own little whiz,
flying closer on snow-angel wings.

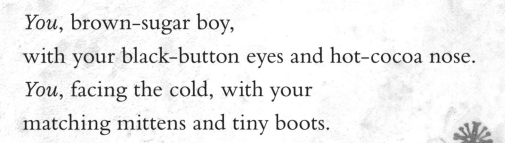

Yes, yes, brown-sugar boy,
you were on your way.
Ready to run outside and play.

You, little one,
were filled with big dreams
of a city sidewalk adventure.

You, Peter, so eager
to make new footprints
in the clean crunchy stuff
beneath your feet.

The time had finally come.
It was 1962.
Ezra Jack Keats dared introduce us to
you.

Peter,
forging your path in knee-deep wonder.
Peter,
welcoming us into your play.
Peter,
marching out in a whole new way.

With *you,* Ezra tore off the blinders.
Yanked up the shades.
Revealed the brilliance
of a brown-bright day.

41

Peter, child,
you brought your stick.
Yes, you did.
Smack-smacked at a tree.
Some say you were whacking
at ice-packed intolerance,
shaking it loose from narrow-
minded branches.

When prejudice fell,
you rolled it, packed it,
put its snowball in your pocket
of possibility,
where it melted away.

Peter and Ezra,
you made a great team.
Together you brought a snowstorm
of dreams.
A blizzard of imagination.
Flurries of fun!

And soon readers called for
more of *where are you?*
And between you two,
the one-of-a-kind snowflakes
kept falling.
Onto sweet pages
of brown-sugar good.

More neighborhood friends.
More books with kids who
answered *where are you?*
with *here we are!*

Yes, yes, there *they* were, too.
Stories with Louie. Roberto. Jennie.
Tales of Amy. Archie. Maggie.
Goggles. A Hat. A Pet Show.
A Chair. Pirates. Skates.
A Man in the Moon.

A doggie named Willie, and
learning to whistle.

A music box for finding a father.
Counting to one
with a red-on-red sun.

Ezra Jack Keats gave all of us a place.
A face.
A voice.

Ezra Jack Keats gave us eyes to see.
Let us celebrate the making
of what it means to *be*.

He dared to open a door.
He awakened a wonderland.
He brought a world of white
suddenly alive with color.

Brown-sugar child,
when *you* and your hue
burst onto the scene,
all of us came out to play.
Together,
flapping our wings,
rejoicing in a *we-all* blanket of *wheeee!*

Thanks to Ezra Jack Keats,
we all can *be*.
As bright as Snow's everlasting wonder.

EZRA'S LEGACY

In 1962, Ezra Jack Keats took a bold leap and never looked back. He'd started his career in children's publishing in 1954 illustrating books written by authors other than himself. Then came an invitation to write and illustrate his own book.

As an artist who had grown up surrounded by poverty and anti-Semitism, Ezra understood what it was like to be excluded. Also, as a man who'd spent much of his life in New York City, he'd seen people from a range of ethnic backgrounds. Yet none of these appeared in the children's books that were being published at that time. Also missing in works of literature for young people were urban settings. Kids who lived among apartment buildings and brownstones, and whose playgrounds were made of concrete and chain-link fences, didn't see the beauty of their urban lives reflected in the picture books they read.

So when the opportunity came to create his own book, Ezra Jack Keats didn't have to think twice about the story's main character. He immediately remembered the series of *Life* magazine photographs that he'd been saving for more than twenty years, for something. The strip of four pictures depicts a black child who is about to get a shot from a doctor. The boy's facial expressions, attitude, clothing, and all-out feisty cuteness are the inspiration for that special something Keats had been waiting to portray. This was the beginning of Keats's *The Snowy Day*, a story set in a city and whose main character, Peter, is African American. This was also the start of Ezra Jack Keats's creative exuberance that would be expressed through his body of work as an author/illustrator. Keats was a master of urban orchestration. His books celebrated the beauties of New York City's neighborhoods. They featured street corners, front stoops, graffiti, manholes, and storefronts. They included black and

Latino children and families, homeless people, and colorful construction workers.

In creating the illustrations for *The Snowy Day,* Keats extended the boundaries of his own creativity by using collage: cutouts of patterned paper, fabrics, and oilcloth. He layered his work with snippets of torn paper and fabrics to create patterns. The papers used for the collage aspects of the paintings echo Keats's desire to create a book that celebrated diversity. They came from Japan, Italy, Sweden, and other countries.

Keats achieved the book's snowy effects with homemade snowflake stamps and with India inks spattered with a toothbrush. In describing the joys of creating *The Snowy Day*'s multifaceted illustrations, Keats said, "I was like a child playing." And he recalled the artistic freedom of being "in a world with no rules."

The editor of *The Snowy Day,* Annis Duff, also pushed past convention. She rejected Keats's first sketch for the book's cover, which featured a large snowman. Duff was emphatic. She told Keats that his "lovely, sympathetic book" must feature Peter prominently on its cover. Putting a black boy front and center on a picture book's jacket was unheard of at that time, but Annis

insisted. Interestingly, the ad copy and the text of the book never mention Peter's race, which speaks to the story's universal celebration of every child having fun.

The Snowy Day is among Keats's most notable books. It was awarded the 1963 Caldecott Medal, and was named one of the 100 Most Important Children's Books of the 20th Century by the New York Public Library.

In his Caldecott speech, Keats said, "I can honestly say that Peter came into being because we wanted him." And Keats reminds us that Peter is timeless because he bestows the "wisdom of a pure heart."

Peter is featured in six more books that were published after *The Snowy Day*, and that follow him as he grows from a little boy to a pre-adolescent. The fifth Peter book, *Goggles!*, published in 1969, received a Caldecott Honor Medal.

Many of the events in Keats's books in addition to Peter's snow-play in *The Snowy Day* are based on his own childhood experiences. Willie, Peter's dog in *Whistle for Willie*, is named after Ezra's older brother. The blind man in the book *Apt. 3* is based on a neighbor who lived downstairs from the Keats family.

As an African American child growing up in the 1960s, at a time when I didn't see others like me in children's books, I was profoundly affected by the expressiveness of Keats's illustrations.

Ezra Jack Keats's work continues to inspire. The Ezra Jack Keats New Writer Award was established in 1985 by the Ezra Jack Keats Foundation, to encourage and celebrate up-and-coming authors of picture books whose stories reflect the universal qualities of childhood and our multicultural world. The Ezra Jack Keats New Illustrator Award was created in 2001 to reward originality of artistic expression.

KEATS, THE COLLAGE POET

Ezra Jack Keats's urban rhythms and the undeniable power of poetry as a storytelling tool are the reasons I have chosen to render Keats's biography as a tribute poem.

The use of a verse narrative to present Keats's life echoes Keats's use of collage to tell a story. *A Poem for Peter* is a portrait that employs a form known as a "collage verse," "bio-poem," or "tapestry narrative" in which factual components are layered with a mix of elements.

In this poem, Peter's presence approaches throughout the story in a "peek-a-boo" fashion, waving at the reader, serving as a narrative thread that is stitched throughout. Peter's presence helps bring us through Ezra Jack Keats's life and times. Young readers come to see how the childhood influences rendered here led Keats to create his most memorable characters and settings.

Also, *A Poem for Peter* shows readers how, as in a tapestry or collage, our families, homes, friends, and experiences shape who we become, and what we bring to the world. Ezra's story, as told here, invites readers of all ages to explore their own "life collages" and to "cut and paste" elements from their personal histories to create poems of their own, or about notable people they admire.

In many respects, Keats was a poet who brought visual cadence to his work. Through his playful use of collage, his books celebrate the rhythms of city living. They invite the eye to dance, and they make his stories accessible.

Books Written and Illustrated by *EZRA JACK KEATS*

*

Keats wrote a total of seven books featuring Peter between 1962 and 1972:

The Snowy Day (1962)

Whistle for Willie (1964)

Peter's Chair (1967)

A Letter to Amy (1968)

Goggles! (1969)

Hi, Cat! (1970)

Pet Show! (1972)

Other books include:

My Dog Is Lost (1960)

John Henry, an American Legend (1965)

Jennie's Hat (1966)

The Little Drummer Boy by Katherine Davis; illustrated by Ezra Jack Keats (1968)

Apt. 3 (1971)

Over in the Meadow by Olive Wadsworth; illustrated by Ezra Jack Keats (1971)

Pssst! Doggie— (1973)

Skates! (1973)

Dreams (1974)

Kitten for a Day (1974)

Louie (1978)

The Trip (1978)

Maggie and the Pirate (1979)

Louie's Search (1980)

Regards to the Man in the Moon (1981)

Clementina's Cactus (1982)

Author Andrea Davis Pinkney celebrates a snowy day in her Brooklyn neighborhood.

ACKNOWLEDGMENTS

It is with special gratitude that I thank the following individuals and institutions for their research assistance and Ezra Jack Keats insights: Martin Pope, lifelong friend of Ezra Jack Keats; Deborah Pope, Ph.D., Executive Director, Ezra Jack Keats Foundation; Ellen Hunter Ruffin, Curator and Associate Professor, The deGrummond Children's Literature Collection; Karen Van Rossem; Morton Schindel, Paul Gagne, and Melissa Reilly Ellard, Weston Woods Studios.

Exceeding thanks to Kenneth Wright, VP and Publisher, Viking, and Regina Hayes, Viking editor extraordinaire, for inviting me to explore the wonders of Keats's life and legacy. And thanks to art director Denise Cronin and designer Nancy Brennan, whose creative visions brought this book alive. Special thanks to artists Steve Johnson and Lou Fancher for their illustrative genius.

SOURCES CONSULTED FOR THE CREATION OF THIS BOOK

＊

Alderson, Brian. *Ezra Jack Keats: Artist and Picture-Book Maker.* Gretna, Louisiana:
Pelican Publishing Co., Inc., 1994.

Cech, John. *Imagination and Innovation: The Story of Weston Woods.* New York: Scholastic Press, 2009.

Engel, Dean, and Florence B. Freedman. *Ezra Jack Keats: A Biography with Illustrations.*
New York: Silver Moon Press, 1995.

Silvey, Anita. Introduction. *Keats's Neighborhood: An Ezra Jack Keats Treasury.* New York: Viking, 2002.

WEBSITES

The Ezra Jack Keats Foundation: www.ezra-jack-keats.org.

The Jewish Museum, New York:
thejewishmuseum.org/exhibitions/the-snowy-day-and-the-art-of-ezra-jack-keats.

RESEARCH COLLECTION ARCHIVAL MATERIALS

The de Grummond Children's Literature Collection, McCain Library and Archives,
University of Southern Mississippi.

INTERVIEWS

Martin Pope, Founder/President, Board of Directors, the Ezra Jack Keats Foundation; Professor Emeritus,
Department of Chemistry, New York University; lifetime friend of Ezra Jack Keats.

Deborah Pope, Ph.D., Executive Director, the Ezra Jack Keats Foundation

Ellen Hunter Ruffin, Curator and Associate Professor, the de Grummond Children's Literature Collection.

＊

The paintings for this book were rendered in acrylic, collage, and pencil on paper,
using images from *The Snowy Day*; *Peter's Chair*; *Hi, Cat*; and *Jennie's Hat*.

VIKING

Penguin Young Readers Group

An imprint of Penguin Random House LLC

375 Hudson Street

New York, New York 10014

First published in the United States of America by Viking, an imprint of Penguin Random House LLC, 2016

LIBRARY OF CONGRESS CATALOGING-IN-PUBLICATION DATA IS AVAILABLE

ISBN 9780425287682

Manufactured in China

1   3   5   7   9   10   8   6   4   2